Miguel Mennig

GW00702932

Search engines

CASSELL&CO

First published in the United Kingdom in 2000 by Hachette UK

ISBN 1 84202 057 9

Designed by Chouka / Typeset in Sabon MT / Printed and bound in Germany

English translation by Prose Unlimited

Concept and editorial direction: Gheorghii Vladimirovitch Grigorieff

Additional editorial assistance: Colette Holden, Andrew Bolton,
   Jeremy Smith, Rachel Catt

A CIP catalogue for this book is available from the British Library.

© English Translation Hachette UK 2000

© Marabout 2000

Hachette UK

Cassell & Co

The Orion Publishing Group

Wellington House

125 Strand

London

WC2R 0BB

Table of Contents

1

Introduction

INTRODUCTION

The Internet is often compared to a gigantic library. At the dawning of the new millennium, there are nearly one billion Web pages, with thousands being added every day. It is estimated that this virtual library will double in volume every eighteen months.

However, unlike a real library, the books or documents are not filed or arranged with any precise classification, and it is pointless to ask the head librarian to guide you through this maze, for the simple reason that the Internet is not subject to any regulating authority. Everyone is free to create his or her site and thus take part in the creation of this much vaunted brave new cyber world.

So what are you to do: wander or 'surf' aimlessly in search of the information you want, looking for a needle in a haystack? In short, this library is useless without the equivalent of a catalogue or an index, hence the importance of search tools. Whether national or international, general or specialised, they have become indispensable tools that help you to make sense of the Web.

That said, many surfers who have tried a search with a given engine are drowned by thousands of replies that have little to do with the information they want. For a search to be effective, it must be neither too specific nor too generalised. To get good results, you must learn how to use these tools.

The purpose of this manual is to help you to get to know and use these tools. Beyond certain general search principles, each tool has different features. Get the hang of them and you will be able to conduct your search with maximum precision.

Access to search tools and techniques will enable you to delve deeper into the Net to find what you desire: last minute flights to Ibiza, cooking recipes, the works of Shakespeare, dictionaries, the music of Bach or Bowie, newspapers online, image databases, updated stockmarket prices, e-mail addresses, etc. The Internet is hell bent on becoming the electronic fountain of all human knowledge and activity.

2

Which tools ?

WHICH TOOLS ?

Search tools can be divided roughly into four major categories: directories, such as Yahoo or UK Plus; 'normal' search engines, such as AltaVista, HotBot or Fast; meta search engines, such as SavySearch or MetaCrawler; and finally theme search engines or directories, such as the Virtual Library. We will go over the general features of these tools and how they can be adapted to suit your needs.

DIRECTORIES

Directories are catalogues of sites classified by categories and subcategories. To conduct a search you can proceed from the general to the particular until you find the subject you want.

For example, to find housing to rent on Yahoo, you may start in *Business and Economy* and wind up in the *Accommodation* section, where you can search by *Region*.

But for a precise search, you can also enter a query using keywords in the search form on the home page.

The main characteristic of directories is that they are based on a human approach. People are employed to assess the sites, therefore the directories are not produced automatically and the assessors may refuse to include a given site because of the paucity of contents, or because of racist or other connotations. Furthermore, it may sometimes take a while for a new site to be indexed.

The volume of directories cannot possibly vie with that of a search engine, as humans cannot comb the Web at the same speed as a robot. But the indexed information is usually more coherent and better structured.

Furthermore, the sites are often annotated, thereby providing an idea as to how relevant they are to the information you want.

Directories are particularly appropriate for a search on a general theme or when the field of search is quite wide. They enable you to familiarise yourself with a subject and its vocabulary, and if you are not entirely happy with the search, this vocabulary will in turn enable you to use keywords to conduct a more specific search with a search engine.

For example, if you are looking for specific solutions to the *Doom* game, it would be best to enter this word directly into a search engine. However, if you are searching for general information on computer games, you would do better to use a directory like Yahoo, starting under the *Entertainment* category, then proceeding under *Computer Games*.

The best known directory is undoubtedly Yahoo, which was designed in 1994 by two students at Stanford University. Apart from having a great name, Yahoo! is available in several different national versions and is said to perform ten million searches each week.

SEARCH ENGINES

A search engine locates requested information in a gigantic database of Web page extracts. The database is compiled by *spiders*, also known as *robots*, automated programs that trawl the Web for new documents and files. No human indexer could ever handle the huge number of new documents that are placed on the Internet every day. Internet surfers activate searches by using keywords.

AltaVista is the most popular of the international engines, but competition remains fierce, as newcomers such as Fast or Google make no bones about their ambitions. Moreover, in addition to general search engines, there are an increasing number of search engines which specialize in a particular field or discipline (newsgroups, law, medicine, IT, etc.).

The enormous databases created are not identical from one search engine to the next. This is not only because of the (ever more astounding) power of the relevant software, but because the exploration and indexing criteria that are applied are different from one search engine to another. Some engines will go through only the title and the home page of a site, while others will conduct a search on the complete text of all the pages. Similarly, the relevance criteria applied to the queries varies, and each search engine uses its own algorithms to try and find relevant pages only.

In any event, no search engine to date indexes the entire Web, and the frequency at which they are updated varies as well. Use these factors to your advantage. If your first search does not yield satisfactory results, don't throw in the towel — simply start again using a different search engine.

Beyond these restrictions, however, the basic problem lies in querying these search engines correctly and making proper use of the many operators and features each has to offer to hone your search. Some basic principles are valid for all searches, regardless of the search engine used, but we shall also explain how some major search engines function in detail.

It is worth noting that all search engines feature help pages for simple and advanced searches. If you work regularly with the same search engine, consult these pages to find out more about them. A detailed search on one or two search engines you are thoroughly familiar with will be more effective than an approximate search on a wide range of engines.

Generally speaking, search engines operate a more extensive database than directories, and will make a much faster inventory of sites. But the content of the sites is not subjected to human verification, and can at times serve up surprises, so you risk being overwhelmed by an avalanche of commercial or other irrelevant sites...

We should finally point out that the distinction between search engines and directories is becoming less and less obvious. Some directories are coupled with a search engine, and many engines include a directory of annotated sites. That said, a search engine will without question yield better results for a well specified query; whereas a directory, with its user-friendly approach, is more appropriate for broader searches.

META SEARCH ENGINES

A meta search engine launches a parallel search on all the main search engines. It then compiles a distillation of the most relevant sites from the results. In this way, your query will be put simultaneously to search engines such as AltaVista, HotBot, Lycos and others, depending on the choice of each meta search engine.

The problem is that each search engine has its own features that the meta search engine will not be able to use. Each search engine is curbed, as it were – stripped of its most advanced features. The search will therefore be more superficial, but in some cases it might prove useful to compare the results and then query directly the search engine which seems to have yielded the most relevant results.

We shall examine in closer detail how three meta search engines operate, namely MetaCrawler, Profusion and SavySearch later in the book (see page 143).

THEME DIRECTORIES OR SEARCH ENGINES

These are search engines or databases set up by universities and other such institutions with 'expert' knowledge. In a particular field such as history, medicine, the environment, law and the economy, sites are selected, evaluated and often commented upon. The volume of information is not comparable to that of other search tools, but the choice and quality of that information make it a particularly reliable source. You do not risk ending up in commercial sites or ditsy personal sites. Examples worth citing include the excellent WWW Virtual Library and Argus Clearinghouse directories. These tools are always recommended if you have to carry out an in-depth search on a particular subject.

3

Search principles

SEARCH PRINCIPLES

There are two major search methods on the Web.

 The first is a search through sites that are classified in categories and subcategories found in directories.

This does not differ all that much, in fact, from a search you would carry out in a large record shop when you want to buy a record. Let us suppose that you are looking for the latest CD by a traditional musician from Mali. You would not waste time under classical or rock music, but would head straight for the world music section. There you would search under Africa, then Mali, and finally the musician in question. The procedure would seem self-evident.

The other search method uses keywords entered in a search form.

When approaching such a search form for the first time, the surfer's immediate reflex is to enter a keyword that should encapsulate his or her query. When the search engine serves up thousands of results, or replies that no matches whatsoever were found, the tendency for the unhappy surfer is to call the search engine all the names under the sun and write it off as a bad job.

However if the surfer perseveres with the search, entering several keywords one after the other in desperation, the search engine may still disappoint, or serve an avalanche of matches which would take hours to sift through.

We must therefore select the keyword or keywords that come closest to the meaning of the query. If you launch a general search on astronomy, you will undoubtedly find tens of thousands of pages dealing with this subject, but you will be swamped with results.

If you enter the word 'star', you must also indicate that sites dealing with *Star Wars* or film stars must be excluded. In this instance, you could also get around the problem by entering the words 'stellar astronomy', but this search would also be too wide. Additional keywords would be needed to hone your search.

In short, whereas it is important to use several well-chosen keywords, it is as important to define a certain logic between them, and that this logic be 'understood' by the search engine. This is where Boolean operators such as AND, OR, NOT, NEAR come into play. These are words or operators, usually in capital letters, that indicate how search terms should be combined to make the search as specific and therefore effective as possible (see page 34).

USING KEYWORDS

Defining the search

This principle is even more relevant when searching on the Internet. The computer cannot understand the subleties of language, so you have to be as specific as possible, defining the principle object of your search and separating out any secondary data that may add confusion to the search.

 Once this principle object has been defined, translate it into the keywords which encapsulate it best.

Check the spelling and the syntax of the search or query

 A query may be perfectly worded, but a simple spelling error is enough to sabotage the whole operation. It is also best to avoid using accents.

2   Use nouns rather than adjectives or adverbs. A search engine often ignores a series of what are known as 'stopwords' such as pronouns, conjunctions, articles, prepositions or terms that are too general such as Web or Internet. Conversely, if you are looking for a precise phrase or expression, such as the title of a book or a film, you must put it between quotation marks including the stopwords:

'The Name of the Rose'

3   Keywords should be put in the singular rather than the plural. Your search will be far more successful, especially as several search engines will look for occurrences of the word in the plural.

Pay attention to word order

4   Some search engines give priority to the keyword placed first in your query, so pay attention to the word order and in general enter the most important word of the query first.

Searching for synonyms

5   A search can turn out fruitless because a word in your query does not correspond to the words indexed by the search engine. It will suffice at times to launch your query again by replacing a word by a synonym.

> So if you are searching for pages on data encryption, you can use the word encryption, coding or encoding. We will see how it is possible to introduce synonyms in the query with the operator 'OR'.

Searching for a phrase

6   In many cases, you will need to search for an exact phrase, such as the title of a book or a film, or an expression composed of several words. If you enter simply the different words one after the other, the search engine may launch a search on each separate word and suggest many documents that have nothing to do with your query. A search on *mad cow disease*, for example, may find a series of matches dealing with many kinds of diseases or dairy cow production!

To launch a search on all the words in the same order, just put the phrase or expression between quotation marks:

'German shepherd', 'mad cow disease'

'Golden Gate Bridge'

'The Name of the Rose'

Use quotation marks as often as possible, as it is an effective method for refining your search.

Stemming

7   Many words have the same stem. You can widen the search by keying in only the stem, followed by a 'joker' or a 'wildcard' to replace one or several characters.

The most common is the asterisk. It is generally used after at least three characters.

engine*

will search for pages containing engine, engineer, engineering and so on.

garden*

will search for pages containing garden, gardening, gardener and so on.

Some search engines feature this option by default and, for instance, search for the terms automatically in plurals.

Less frequently, the % or ? sign is used to replace a single character inside a word. The Northern Light search engine, for example, recognises the joker %.

@ **Sara%evo**

will therefore search for pages containing Sarajevo or Sarayevo.

Be careful, because using the asterisk may launch a search on words you had not thought of.

Case

8 A search engine is said to be case sensitive if it makes a difference between the use of lowercase and uppercase characters. Some search engines are not case sensitive and will yield the same results for the words *windows* and *Windows*.

In general you should use an initial uppercase letter for proper names only. Also, if it is a name or proper noun, put it between quotation marks:

'Bill Gates', 'New York Times', 'Windows 98'

Conversely, enter Boolean operators entirely in uppercase:

AND, OR...

BOOLEAN OPERATORS

The term 'Boolean' comes from the mathematician George Boole (1815–1864), who founded a branch of mathematics based on all operations producing just two values, true or false.

9   Used in queries, the Boolean operators, or words, AND, OR or NOT (or AND NOT, depending on the search engine) enable you to specify and limit considerably the scope of the search by defining logical relationships between keywords. They can also be combined with parentheses for more complex searches.

In the detailed analysis of the different search engines that follows, we shall describe how to use these operators. Some search engines, for instance, use drop-down menus that offer options equivalent to Boolean operators.

> In general, Boolean operators are written in uppercase with a space on either side of the operator.

OR

This operator widens the search to all documents containing *at least one* of the terms of the query:

vanilla OR chocolate

It is used frequently to link synonyms or neighbouring concepts:

old OR retired

Macintosh OR Apple

If you use only one of the two terms (Apple, for example), you may not obtain relevant documents containing the term Macintosh.

This operator can also be used to enter a word spelled in two different ways:

color OR colour

Peking OR Beijing

These examples will make sure you do not miss documents containing one or the other spelling.

`AND`

This operator restricts the search to documents containing all the terms of the query. Contrary to what you might suppose at first glance, a search with AND is more restrictive than a search with OR, since both the terms must be present in the documents.

> man AND woman will find fewer matches than man OR woman.

Several search engines also accept the plus sign (+), without a space between the words on either side:

+man +woman

However, the fact that the two terms are found in the same document does not necessarily mean they are associated. They can be in different sections and not be related to each other.

NOT
(or AND NOT for Excite or AltaVista)

This operator restricts the search by excluding documents containing the word excluded from the query.

Mac OR Apple NOT pie,

excludes documents dealing with apple pie.

star NOT wars

excludes documents dealing with Star Wars.

Several search engines also accept the minus sign (–) without a space between it and the next term:

+star-wars

+turkey-country

NEAR

Used less frequently than the others, NEAR requires the presence of both the terms concerned, but also entails a defined proximity between them, i.e. they must not be separated by more than a certain number of words. Some engines set a default value: AltaVista insists that the two terms cannot be separated by more than 10 words. Others let you specify the maximum distance. The operator is followed by a slash and the desired number (without a space) :

caste NEAR India

caste NEAR/20 India

This function may prove useful if you do not want a search with AND to yield pages where the two words of the query are found in different contexts.

Note

At times, however, quotation marks may turn out to be even more effective:

drift NEAR continental

will be less precise than

'continental drift'

Several engines let you launch a Boolean search by using menus or buttons. For instance, for AND, you may find the option '*all the words*' while the equivalent for OR would be '*any*'. You will thus launch a Boolean search, but without direct recourse to these operators.

Before you conduct a search, it is important to know which operator the engine uses by default.

PARENTHESES AND NESTING

10   If you launch a more complex search using several operators, you can use parentheses to specify the logical relations between them and to make the query more 'legible' for the search engine.

If you use OR and AND, for example, you should put the terms linked by OR between parentheses:

(cats OR felines) AND behaviour

will search for documents containing *behaviour* and at least one of the two other terms. The pages should pertain to the behaviour of cats or felines in general.

(delinquency OR crime) AND (juvenile OR teenagers OR minors) NOT 'European Community'

will launch a search on juvenile delinquency, but not in the European Community.

Be careful when using parentheses, however, and do not complicate matters unnecessarily. The simpler your wording, the easier it will be for the search engine to interpret it. For instance, you can simplify the previous query and check whether the results are relevant, and in certain cases, rather than exclude a term with NOT, it would be better to specify the term you want with AND:

'juvenile delinquency' AND Russia

When you enter parentheses, do not use + or – signs but the operators AND, OR.

FIELD LIMITERS

11 A search may not necessarily pertain to an entire document or all Web sites. You may, for example, want to find an image or you may want the object of your query to be contained in the title, not within the text of a page. Alternatively, your search may be more effective if limited to a single Web domain (.gov, .edu, .com).

There are tools available for this type of specification called 'field limiters'. You may enter these into the search form and may or may not want to combine them with keywords and Boolean operators.

The main ones are given below. Search engines do not on the whole accept them, but when we explain the main search engines separately, we will indicate which limiters are permitted.

 Warning: you must not enter a space between the limiter, the colon and the next term!

anchor:

searches for pages with text specifying a precise link.

anchor:click here to visit AltaVista

searches for pages containing the link thus defined.

applet:

searches for pages containing the defined applet.

domain:

restricts the search to the selected domain (edu, com, fr, uk).

+Einstein+domain:edu

searches for Einstein in edu only.

+football+domain:fr

searches for football in French pages only.

host:

searches the pages of the defined server.

+ecology+host:BBC

searches the pages on ecology hosted on the BBC server.

image:

searches for pages containing the defined image.

image:Einstein

searches for pages containing an image of Einstein.

link:

searches for pages containing the defined link.

link:altavista. com

searches for pages with a link to AltaVista.

text:

searches for the word defined in the text (not in images, URLs or links).

text:Einstein

searches for pages with Einstein in the body of the text.

title:

restricts the search to the title of a page only.

title:Einstein

searches only for pages with Einstein in the title.

url:

searches for addresses containing a defined word.

url:einstein

searches for pages with Einstein in the address.

SOME TIPS

Many searches prove fruitless because of a simple typing or spelling error in the query, so double check before you launch the search!

Avoid using terms that are too general. For instance, rather than launching a search on *painting, Renaissance* and *Italy*, try a query such as:

Botticelli AND Vinci AND Michelangelo

Placing a sequence of words (a phrase or expression) between quotation marks makes the query precise and often avoids more complex wording. For example, if you are looking for documentation on global warming, instead of using several key words, why not simply stick to:

'global warming' or 'greenhouse effect' ?

If you find no relevant result in the first ten or twenty matches, there is little chance of finding any matches further down, so do not waste your time going through them. Check the wording of your query instead, and try to make it more specific.

If you do find a relevant result, however, the page in question often provides interesting links to other relevant pages. You should explore them, because they may well spare you the effort of useless searching.

If your priority is to look for a page dealing with the subject of your query, the field limiter *title*: enables you to search only for pages which contain the subject in the title. You will therefore avoid any pages where the term is contained in an isolated spot in the text:

title: 'mad cow'

will search for pages where 'mad cow' is contained in the title.

It is better to use one or two search engines you are thoroughly familiar with than to flit from one to another. If you do not have any keywords for your search, then use a directory such as Yahoo and proceed through the themed categories. You will thus manage to better define your subject, and you can then use a search engine with a few of the keywords you have discovered to conduct a more specific search.

Every search engine or directory has a search HELP feature. There is nothing like it for picking up an additional trick or two. The time spent reading this online help will stand you in good stead for your subsequent searches.

4

General search engines

GENERAL SEARCH ENGINES
WORLD WIDE

This selection of a few powerful world-wide search engines is far from exhaustive. Some, such as AltaVista or Lycos are veterans. Others, such as Northern Light or Fast are relative newcomers who make no bones about their ambition to upset the existing hierarchy. It is for you to judge which search engines are best.

We have always opted for the UK version of an engine when available, but if you prefer the original North-American version, it does not matter as the features of the search engine are nearly identical.

AltaVista

http://www.altavista.co.uk

Launched in 1995 by Digital Equipment and since acquired by Compaq, AltaVista is without question the most famous search engine for seasoned surfers. Long the reference par excellence, today it faces keener competition than ever. A UK version of the search engine was launched in 1999.

In addition to an impressive, constantly updated database, AltaVista boasts a full array of features to help you make elaborate searches. Moreover, it can carry out specific searches in discussion groups (newsgroups) and in multimedia files, and includes many other resources (free e-mail, daily news, customised home pages, etc.).

It also gives you access to the important Open Directory, which is featured on many other engines such as HotBot or Netscape.

The home page presents a simple search form with advanced options such as *Advanced search* or *Images, Audio & Video* (multimedia search).

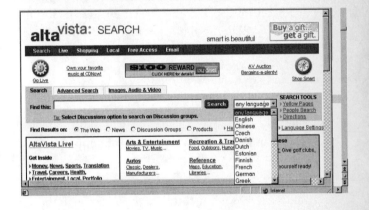

Simple search

The first step consists of choosing the language for your search. The drop-down menu to the right of the **Search** button features 25 languages, including English, French, German, Spanish and Portuguese, with 'any language' set by default. Click this drop-down menu and choose the language you want.

Under the entry screen, 'radio' buttons enable you to gear your search to the Web (default), News, Discussion groups (newsgroups) or Shopping.

AltaVista recognises simple questions in simple language. Do not forget to add the question mark (?). Where possible, it is preferable to use precise key-words for your query, unless your questions are as simple as *What is the capital of Pakistan?*

By default, AltaVista considers keywords implicitly linked by OR. It therefore yields pages containing at least one of the terms of your query:

Blair Jospin

   searches for pages containing Blair or Jospin or both.

If you must have a particular word or an expression in the documents you are searching for, put a plus sign (+) before it, without a space. Similarly, a word or expression preceded immediately by a minus sign (–) will be excluded from your search:

+Blair-Jospin Clinton

   searches for pages containing Blair and Clinton but not Jospin.

To search for a precise string of words or for an expression, use quotation marks:

'Eyes Wide Shut', 'Financial Times'

An asterisk (*) in a word (after at least three characters) or at the end of a word replaces between zero and five characters:

medicin*

will find items containing medicine, medicines, medicinal, etc.

A keyword entered in lowercase will search for all the occurrences of the word in lowercase or upper-case, whereas the same word with one uppercase character will yield only that form of the word:

Turkey

will yield only pages concerning the country, whereas

turkey

will yield pages containing the words turkey and Turkey.

You can limit the search to specific fields. AltaVista recognises the following limiters: anchor, applet, domain, host, image, link, text, title, url.

Advanced search

In addition to the simple search features, the advanced search allows Boolean operators as well as a selection of documents organised by date.

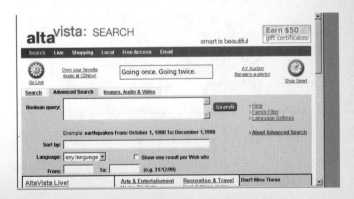

Boolean query

AND or & can be used to search for pages containing all the terms entered.

OR or | can be used to search for pages containing at least one of the terms entered.

AND NOT or ! excludes pages containing the term placed after the operator.

The operator **NEAR** between two terms searches for pages where the two terms are not more than 10 characters away from each other.

Parentheses are used for 'nesting':

(stars OR galaxies) AND 'space research' AND NOT planets

From, to.

This determines the order by which the relevant documents will be displayed.

Sort by

The term entered in this window will determine the documents placed at the top of the results. For example, if for the previous query we were to enter *Hubble* in this window, the documents corresponding to the query and containing this term will be first in the list of matches.

Search for discussion groups (Usenet)

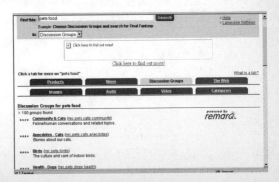

AltaVista also lets you launch searches on more than 30,000 discussion groups and enables you to take part in them.

You can access them in two ways, either from the home page by activating the **DISCUSSIONS** radio button under the entry window, or after a search on the Web, by clicking **DISCUSSION GROUPS** at the top of the page of matches.

A query with quotation marks or + and – signs will create a search relating only to messages posted in the groups and not to the actual names of groups. If you want to find a particular group, just enter one or two keywords.

You will then get a page with the results containing a list and a brief description of the groups dealing with the subject you want.

Click on the name of one of the groups to obtain the page with the relevant subjects, the most recent of which will be placed at the top of the list.

Click on the selected subject to obtain relevant messages. You can reply to a message or search for a new topic by clicking **Start a New Discussion**, but bear in mind the topic of the group concerned. It would not be very tactful to launch a discussion on the beauty of hunting in an ecological group... Also, to take part in these discussions you will have to obtain a login from AltaVista first.

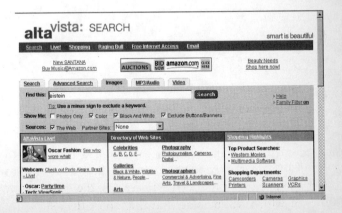

Multimedia search

To conduct a multimedia search, click the **Images, Audio & Video** tabs on the home page.

Depending on the tab you select, you will then activate a drop-down menu placed under the **Images, Audio, Video** entry screen.

You can, for example, select the **Images tab**, and then define your search by keying in photos or graphics, black and white or colour and specifying the format type.

The search functions are the same as for the simple search on the Web, but there are only five field limiters: *domain*, *host*, *media*, *title*, *url*.

Searches for images and videos yield a page with images in thumbnail format. Click on them to access the page containing the image and also a series of additional options. Under each photo, click on **more info** for additional information on the selected source.

 A search for audio files yields a page with a list of files and information on the size, format, copyright, etc. Click on the address to access the selected file.

Einstein.jpg
180x328 27 KB
more info

Einstein-x-sm.jpg
83x83 2 KB
more info

Einstein46.jpg
260x309 13 KB
more info

Remarks

 If your search covers a sufficiently wide field, a heading above the results entitled '**More info**' will provide a series of keywords or concepts related to your query. Just click one of them to launch a new search.

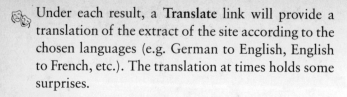

Under each result, a **Translate** link will provide a translation of the extract of the site according to the chosen languages (e.g. German to English, English to French, etc.). The translation at times holds some surprises.

AltaVista groups the different pages of the same site. Click 'More pages from this site' to access the other pages.

The results page enables you to restart the same search, but in another section, by clicking **Images, Audio & Video, Discussion Groups,** or **News** at the top of the page.

Excite UK

http://www.excite.co.uk

Created in 1993 by students at Stanford University, Excite combines the advantages of a search engine with those of a directory.

Excite is distinguished by the fact that it will search for documents not only on the basis of the keywords of the query but also by associated concepts. These are extracted thanks to the ICE (Intelligent Concept Extraction) technique. For instance, the expression 'elderly persons' will extract the concept 'pensioners'.

The different services of Excite include the latest news in different fields (News Channels), directories of professional bodies and private individuals, the weather forecast for cities of your choice, customisation of layout and contents and even your daily horoscope.

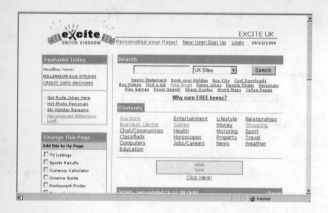

Simple search

By default, the search is conducted only on UK sites. Click on the drop-down menu to launch a search on the Entire Web, European Sites, Excite channels or to launch a News Search.

Operators

 By default, Excite places the operator OR between the keywords of your query. It can therefore yield pages that contain only one keyword. Pages containing several keywords will always be placed at the top of the results.

A query such as **Chirac Blair**, equivalent to **Chirac OR Blair**, will yield first pages that contain both names (if available), followed by pages containing one or other name.

 Excite recognises Boolean operators such as AND, OR or AND NOT as well as parentheses.

Chirac AND Blair

will yield only pages containing the two.

+Chirac +Blair

will yield the same result.

Chirac AND NOT Blair

will yield only pages containing Chirac.

Chirac –Blair

will yield the same result.

Chirac AND (Blair OR Clinton)

will yield pages containing Chirac and Blair, Chirac and Clinton and Chirac, Blair and Clinton.

- Excite recognises quotation marks ('expression sought') and will search the exact character string.

  Thus, mad cow without quotation marks yields 10,082 matches, whereas 'mad cow' yields only 1512.

- Also worth noting are the different guides and directories arranged in 21 topics. They include listings on the subject, specific news, Excite favourites and other resources. It is like a kind of specialised magazine.

Results

The results are displayed by order of relevance, with a percentage for each. The higher the percentage, the more reliable the result. Consequently, if the first addresses are not satisfactory, the odds are that the subsequent ones will not be either.

If you want all the pages of the same site to be grouped, click **List by Web Site**.

Excite suggests a series of terms related to your query in the window entitled **Add related words** to help you to refine your next search. All you have to do is tick one or more of these words and restart the search to include these new keywords.

Every document title is followed by a link entitled **More Like This**. If a document seems particularly relevant, this link will enable you to launch a new search that will use the selected document as reference. It is at times far more useful to proceed in this way than to consult all the results.

Power search

Click the **Power Search** link under the Search button to obtain the power search form.

Boolean operators and quotation marks are not recognised here, but several drop-down menus enable you to hone your search.

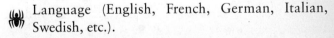

Describe what you want to find...

I want to search	English ▾
in the following domains	UK Sites ▾
My search results MUST contain	the word(s) ▾
My search results MUST NOT contain	the word(s) ▾
My search results CAN contain	the word(s) ▾

● Display my results by document with titles & summaries ▾ and 10 ▾ results per page.

○ Display the top 40 results grouped by web site.

TIP: Do NOT use quotation marks, modifiers like '+' and '-' or operators like 'AND' in this form.
A phrase is a group of two or more words that form a unit based on the exact order in which they appear, e.g. seven wonders of the world

[Search]

- Language (English, French, German, Italian, Swedish, etc.).

- Domain (UK sites, French, European, South American, world wide, etc.).

🕷 The equivalent of the Boolean AND is obtained by entering the words or the segment (phrase or expression) in the box entitled: **My search results MUST contain...**

🕷 The equivalent of AND NOT in Excite is obtained by entering the words or segment (phrase or expression) in the box entitled: **My search results MUST NOT contain...**

🕷 The equivalent of OR is obtained by entering the words or segment (phrase or expression) in the box entitled: **My search results CAN contain...**

🕷 In the drop-down menu, do not forget to activate **the phrase** if you are looking for a string of words or an expression such as **Wall Street Journal**.

Remarks

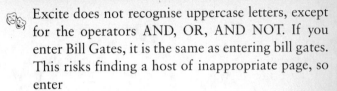

Excite does not recognise uppercase letters, except for the operators AND, OR, AND NOT. If you enter Bill Gates, it is the same as entering bill gates. This risks finding a host of inappropriate page, so enter

'Bill Gates'

instead (with quotation marks), to obtain better results.

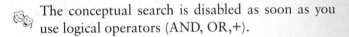

The conceptual search is disabled as soon as you use logical operators (AND, OR,+).

FAST SEARCH (AllTheWeb)

http://www.alltheweb.com

Based in Norway, this search engine is still in its infancy. It was launched in May 1999, in co-operation with Dell. But with a coverage of more than 200 million pages, it is holding its own against competitors and makes no bones about its ambition to cover all the Web.

Despite this phenomenal indexing power, its interface is one of the most succinct, but offers few search features. It has no advanced search, so all the more reason to make the most of the featured techniques and capitalise to the maximum on the 200 million indexed pages. This search engine is surprisingly fast, as its name suggests.

On the whole, however, FAST does not lend itself to complex searches.

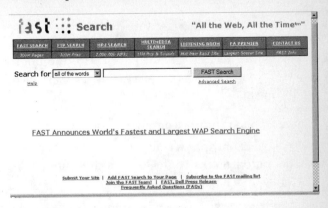

Search

The home page presents a simple form with a drop-down menu featuring three options. Although FAST does not recognise the Boolean operators AND, OR, NOT, it does recognise the + and – signs to include or exclude a term from the query. It also recognises quotation marks for a string of words.

`all the words`

This is the default value, equivalent to the Boolean AND. All the words of the query must be contained in the documents.

Beethoven 'ninth symphony' discography

will yield only pages containing the three terms (the quotation marks confer on 'ninth symphony' the value of a single term).

But the query with a minus sign:

Beethoven -'ninth symphony' discography

will yield only pages containing the discography of Beethoven, excluding those containing the ninth symphony.

any of the words

Equivalent to the **OR** operator, this option will yield documents containing at least one word of your query.

Beethoven 'ninth symphony' discography
will yield documents containing at least one of the terms – including thousands of pages containing for example the discography of the Beatles or Prince...

Beethoven 'ninth symphony ' —discography
will yield pages with Beethoven or the ninth symphony, but without discography.

Beethoven +'ninth symphony ' —discography
will yield the pages where the ninth symphony and perhaps Beethoven must appear, but without a discography.

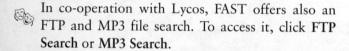

the exact phrase

This allows a search on a phrase or a title of a book or film. This is the equivalent of a phrase between quotation marks in other search engines.

Remark

In co-operation with Lycos, FAST offers also an FTP and MP3 file search. To access it, click **FTP Search** or **MP3 Search**.

For more details, see the Multimedia section in the chapter on Specific Searches (page 173).

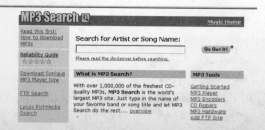

Google

http://www.google.com

The fruit of research conducted at Stanford University, Google has been received with acclaim since it was officially launched in September 1999. Simplicity and precision characterise this search engine which does not (yet) aspire to cover as many pages as its competitors but is distinguished by a number of other traits. For instance, it keeps in memory all the indexed pages, so that you can get a quick idea of the relevance of the search results without having to make a detour through the selected site.

During a search, it also offers to take you immediately to the best site which has been found, rather than wait for results to be displayed. These search results benefit from the GoogleScout, a wizard that suggests a series of sites related to your search.

To measure the 'value' of the sites, Google takes into account the number and importance of the links pointing to them. Given the growing volume of pages on the Web (thousands of pages are added each day), Google has opted for quality and relevance rather than quantity of information.

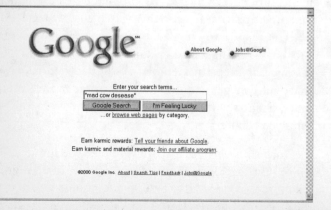

Finally, it is worth noting the surprising speed with which the results are yielded. The search time is always indicated (e.g. 0.26 sec) above the results.

Presentation

Google offers only one search mode, and the interface is one of the most concise, with three functions on offer.

1 To the right of the search form, a drop-down menu displays **10 results**. This is the default value of the number of results per page. You can set this value to 30 or 100.

2 **Google Search** represents the usual button for starting the search and displaying the results.

3 Click **I'm feeling lucky** to start the search. Here, instead of listing the results, Google refers you immediately to the page it considers to be the most relevant to your query, i.e. the one at the top of the results. If the query is sufficiently well worded, you just might be lucky.

Search

 By default, Google automatically uses the operator AND to link the keywords of your query. These must figure in the documents found.

If you want to enter several terms that must figure jointly in the search, just enter them one after the other without any operator or sign.

For example, a search on Blair and Jospin, where both terms must appear, is formulated simply as:

Blair Jospin

 For an expression or phrase, place it between quotation marks:

'mad cow'

 Google ignores certain words of the query, such as very common words or articles. However, these are relevant if inside a phrase or expression you have placed between quotation marks. For Google to consider these words too, you must place a + sign right in front of them without a space. If for example you are searching for information on the Tour de France or the Statue of Liberty, you must enter:

'Tour +de France'

'statue +of liberty'

To exclude a word or expression (between quotation marks) from the search, you must place the – sign immediately before it:

Chirac –Jospin

Google is not case sensitive. The preceding query is equivalent to:

chirac –jospin

If a page seems particularly relevant, all its links probably will be as well. To obtain them, just enter the selected address preceded by **link**. For example, to find pages with a link to www.thing.edu, you must enter:

link:www. thing. edu

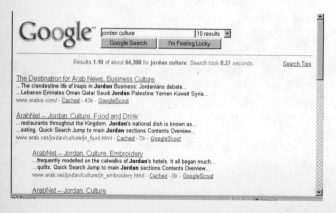

Remarks

 The search results are presented in order of relevance. Each title is followed by an excerpt of the document containing at least one of the words sought, not simply the first lines of the page, as is often the case with other search engines. This means that you can get an inkling of the relevance of the page without having to open up the link first.

 Google keeps a copy of the indexed pages in memory. When you click **cached**, you access these pages faster than the online site. However, the cached version will date from the last indexing, so for queries concerning news, it is best to go directly to the selected page.

 Each address provides you with an opportunity to find related pages. To access them, click on **Google Scout**.

HotBot

www.hotbot.com

Created in 1996 on the initiative of Inktomi and Wired Digital (of *Wired* magazine fame), and acquired by Lycos in 1998, HotBot is distinguished by a particularly flexible and easy-to-use interface and results of relatively high relevance. Its drop-down menus and numerous tick options can be used to conduct complex searches while doing away with the subtleties of a Boolean search. However, Boolean search is also possible in the advanced menu, for those who prefer this approach.

Moreover, HotBot features various types of searches: e-mail, newsgroups, images, sound, video, MP3, Shockwave, VRML and others. Furthermore, you can restrict the search to a domain (.com, .edu), a language or a country.

Finally, the home page features the main categories of what is called the Open Directory, which you can explore by selecting subcategories. This imposing directory is also used by Lycos and AltaVista and represents something of a benchmark in directories.

Simple search

When you enter the selected keywords, HotBot enables you to define, on the left of the screen, different settings from drop-down menus or checkboxes.

Look for

🕷 By default, the search is carried in **all the words** mode. All the keywords are implicitly connected by the operator AND and must all appear in the search results. The query **Chirac Blair** will yield only documents containing these two words.

🕷 Click on the drop-down menu to access the second option: **any of the words**. All the keywords are implicitly linked by OR, and one of them at least must appear in the search results. At the head of the results, you will find those containing the most keywords. The query **Chirac Blair** will yield documents containing at least one of the two terms.

🕷 The third option in this menu — **exact phrase** — is used to search for a phrase or expression in the exact order you have worded it. On other search engines, this is done by putting the phrase between quotation marks.

The query **Last Tango in Paris** will yield pages dealing only with the film, and not with the technique of the dance or tourism in Paris.

Date

By default, the option **anytime** does not take account of the date of the document, but you can use the drop-down menu to specify this (**in the last week, in the last month,** and so on). In the case of a search on a news item, it is often important to obtain relatively recent documents and to specify a deadline.

Language

By default, the search is conducted without a specific language criterion (the default is: **any language**), but you can choose a language for the search in the drop-down menu (English, French, German, Spanish, etc.).

Pages must include

Four checkboxes enable you to specify what you are looking for: **image**, **video**, **MP3** or **JavaScript**.

Return results

By default, the results will be displayed in groups of 10, and each result has some sort of a description. You can choose between a **detailed description** (up to 100 words), a **brief description** or to display **URLs only**.

Advanced search

The simple search mode already offers a series of options which, in many cases, should suffice for a normal search. The advanced search retains these options and adds others, the main ones being:

Look for

In addition to the simple search options, the drop-down menu enables you to search for a **page title, a person, links to this URL** or the use of Boolean operators (**Boolean phrase**).

The latter option will delight those who swear by Boolean search.

HotBot also recognises the symbol **&** or **+** instead of **AND**, the symbol **|** instead of **OR** and the symbol **!** or **−** instead of **NOT**.

Europe AND (Blair OR Jospin)

These operators are obviously compatible with parentheses for a more complex search:

Language

By default, any available language may be selected, as in the simple search, with the same options.

Word Filter

This option enables you to specify words, a phrase or a person that the search results must contain, must not contain, or should, if at all possible, contain.

The option **more terms** enables you to limit the search even more by excluding or including other data.

Date

In addition to the simple search options, you can specify a precise date before or after which a page must have been published.

Date
Limit results to pages published within a specified period of time.

- ◉ anytime ▾
- ○ After ▾ or on
  January ▾ 1 , 1999 ▾

Pages Must Include
Return only pages containing the specified media types or technologies.

- ☐ image ☐ audio ☐ MP3 ☐ video
- ☐ Shockwave ☐ Java ☐ JavaScript ☐ ActiveX
- ☐ VRML ☐ Acrobat ☐ VB Script ☐ Win Media
- ☐ RealAudio/Video ☐ extension: ____ (.gif)

Pages Must Include

This option enables you to obtain only pages containing special files: images, sounds, video, MP3, Shockwave, Acrobat, VRML and others. Just click on the appropriate checkbox(es).

Location/Domain

The **Location** button enables you to select only pages from a given region: North America, Europe, Africa, and so on. The **Domain** button enables you to limit the search to a Web domain (.com, .edu...) or a country (.uk, .fr, .es, etc.). If you are not sure about a country code, click the **domain and country** index for a list.

Page Depth

This option enables you to specify the level of search in a site. The information you are looking for should be on the **Top Page**, the level you specify, or on **Any page** (default value)?

For instance, if you are searching for a site focused on the subject of your query, this subject will probably figure on the first page and there would be no point in conducting a more advanced search.

Word stemming

If you tick **Enable word stemming**, HotBot will find documents with grammatical variants of the keywords. For instance, the keyword *inventor* will yield pages with *invention*, *invent*, *inventors*.

It is worth pointing out that, for stemming purposes, HotBot recognises the asterisk and the question mark in any point of the word.

The asterisk replaces zero or several characters:

huma*

will yield pages with *human*, *humane*, *humanity*, etc.

The question mark replaces a single character:

 feminis?

will yield *feminism* or *feminist*.

Remarks

If you enter a keyword in lowercase letters, HotBot will search for all the occurrences of the word, whether in lowercase or uppercase. For example:

jaguar

will yield pages containing *jaguar*, *Jaguar* and *JAGUAR*.

Jaguar

will yield pages that contain *Jaguar* only.

 HotBot can also conduct searches on discussion groups (newsgroups) with *Deja.com*. Just click on **Discussion Groups**, under the search form.

You may then enter a question or a topic. For a more advanced search, click on **Power Search** to search by discussion group, author, subject or date. You can access this service directly at

http://www.hotbot.com/usenet

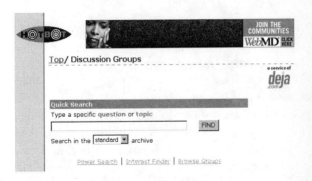

 If a page among the search results seems particularly relevant, click on **Search these results** to start a new search which will take account of your choice and yield the closest pages.

HotBot recognises the field limiters *title* and *domain*:

Einstein domain:edu

searches for pages containing *Einstein* in the domain **edu** only.

Lycos

http://www.lycos.co.uk

Designed at Carnegie Mellon University in 1994, Lycos is another memorable 'old' search engine that has since turned into a real portal with numerous services that can enrich the search (e-mail, weather forecast, customised page, telephone directory, news). Above all, it now provides powerful modules for a specific search, helping you to find FTP, MP3, images or video by simply checking the relevant boxes.

You can also find a site directory divided into 28 categories. These *Web guides* feature numerous specialised resources.

Today, Lycos is available in 13 national versions.

Simple search

🕷 The search interface is one of the most simple. At the top of the screen is the search window, where you enter the terms of the query, and to the right the **Go Get It!** key to start the search.

Under this window, there are two radio buttons for a search on **UK & Ireland** or on **The Web**.

🕷 By default, Lycos considers the terms of the search to be linked by AND. To have the search conducted on all the terms of the query, just enter these words one after the other.

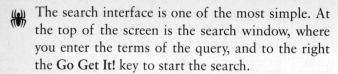

Blair Jospin

searches for documents containing the two terms.

🕷 To exclude a term from the search, put a minus (–) sign right before it.

Clinton -Lewinsky

searches for documents containing Clinton but not Lewinsky.

To search for an exact word string, place it between quotation marks.

'**Massive Attack**'

will yield only documents in which the two words are side by side.

Search options

Click **Search Options** under the simple search window.

News
Pictures of the Day
Weather

Music @ CDNow
BT
LOOT
Thomson Directories
Travel service
Books @ BOL.com
Mortgages with John
Charcol

Business Directory
Classifieds
Buy your Domain
Jobs
Pictures & Sound
Search Options
Translation
Who supplies what?

Search Options

Search for [   ]   *Quick Reference*

[All the words (any order) ▼]   Find !

What catalog?

○ The Web   ○ Pictures   ○ Books
○ UK & Ireland Sites   ○ Sounds   ○ MP3 Files
○ Tripod Homepages

What part?

○ Entire document   ○ selected website:
○ Title only   [   ]
○ URLs only   for example: dizney.com or MIT.edu

What language?

15 languages to choose from: [All ▼]

What is relevant to you?

Match all words...	high ▼	Close together...	medium ▼
Frequency of words...	medium ▼	Appear in title...	medium ▼
Near beginning of text	medium ▼	In exact order...	medium ▼

Enter the keywords in the text field, and then go to the drop-down menu (situated below this field) which features several search options:

All the words (any order), the default value, searches for pages that must contain all the terms entered. This is equivalent to a search with the operator AND, which you can also use, incidentally. Other options enable you to specify word order and the proximity of words to each other.

Any of the words is equivalent to a search with the operator OR, which is also recognised.

Natural language enables you to ask a question as a proper sentence, as you might ask another person.

The Exact Phrase searches for a word string identical to that in the query. This is equivalent to placing this string between quotation marks, likewise authorised.

Note that you can also use the operator **NOT** to exclude a word or expression.

What catalog enables you to specify the scope of the search by means of radio buttons.

By default, the search is carried out on **The Web**, but you can restrict it to **UK & Ireland Sites** or to **Tripod Homepages**.

You can also conduct a search on **Pictures, Sounds, Books** or **MP3 Files**.

The **What part** menu specifies whether the search is to be carried out on the **Entire document** (default), **Title only, URLs only** or a **selected website**. In the latter case, you must enter the address of the site.

What language is used to specify the language of the sites to be searched. Fifteen languages are available, including English, French, German and Italian. The default option is **All**.

The **What is relevant to you** menu is used to weigh the importance of the criteria applied, to establish the order in which to present the results.

Three values (**high, medium, low**) are available for defining these criteria. The appearance of the keywords in the title or at the top of the page may prove particularly significant for your search. By granting a high value to these criteria, any corresponding pages will appear at the top of the results.

The **How to display the results** menu is used to specify the number of results displayed on a page (10 to 40) or to indicate whether the results must be arranged by domain or by order of relevance.

Remarks

 The results page displays a window in which you can refine your search by entering an additional keyword or expression, or launch a new search without going back to the home page. You can also conduct the same search again from this page, but this time on other categories. All you have to do is click on one of the links on offer, i.e. **UK and Ireland sites, The Web, Books** or **Sounds or Pictures**.

The results of a search on sounds or pictures specify the file format for each of the matches (AU, MPE, wav, mid, jpg, tiff, etc).

Lycos is not case sensitive. The query *turkey* or *Turkey* will yield the same results.

My Lycos offers you a customised home page. You can customise the **Content, Layout** and **Colours** to appear in your Personal Guide. For instance, in News, you can tick Politics, Business, Sports or Pictures of the Day. The choice available is really very wide.

Northern Light

http://www.nlsearch.com

http://www.northernlight.com

This search engine ranks among the top three in terms of the number of pages indexed, and boasts many search features (such as search by domain, language or country) which make it a complete tool.

It also has many distinctive features, such as *Custom Search Folder* (which groups the results into folders) and *Special Collection*, a parallel search on documents from more than 5600 different sources (newspapers, magazines, press agencies, etc.). More than 12 million documents are available (for $1.00 to $4.00 depending on the source). Northern Light also offers a free service, notifying you by e-mail about new developments on topics you have selected (*Search Alert Service*), whether in a site or a publication.

This function should be of great interest to all those who closely monitor new developments in their discipline, such as doctors or researchers.

In short, this is a search engine that is becoming more popular by the day.

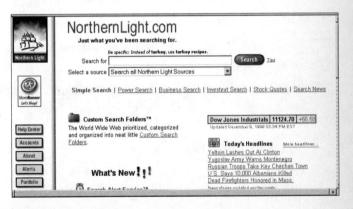

Simple search

🕷 A drop-down menu under the query window enables you to define the contents for your search.

All Sources is the default value. The search is carried out on the Web and all other resources (Special Collection).

World Wide Web restricts the search to the Web.

Special collection restricts the search to resources collected by Northern Light.

🕷 Northern Light recognises the Boolean operators AND (or the + sign), OR, NOT (or the − sign) as well as parentheses. Consequently, the query

(Blair OR Jospin) AND Europe

will search for documents that must contain Europe and at least one of the other two terms.

🕷 By default, Northern Light will search for pages containing all the words entered in the query, as if preceded by AND.

To search for a phrase or expression, place it between quotation marks:

mad cow or (mad cow) yields 63,264 results whereas `mad cow' yields only 27,967.

An asterisk replaces one or more characters. It must follow a minimum of four characters:

invest*

will yield documents containing *investing*, *investment*, *investor*, etc.

The % sign, placed after a minimum of four characters, replaces a single character:

feminis%

will search for documents containing *feminist* and *feminism*.

This function can be useful when searching for a word with an uncertain or alternative spelling:

Sara%evo

will search for documents containing *Sarayevo* or *Sarajevo*.

It is also worth pointing out that Northern Light searches automatically for the words of the query in the singular and in the plural.

If you are searching for a page whose title contains a defined word, put 'title' (without a space) before it:

title:Beatles

will yield pages whose titles contains the word *Beatles*.

Similarly, if you are searching for a page whose address (URL) contains a defined word, put 'url' before it:

url:Beatles

will yield pages whose URL contains the word *Beatles*.

Power search

In addition to the search options defined in the simple search, you can carry out an advanced search, accessed by selecting the Power Search option (see next screenshot).

There are two parts to the Power Search window:

You can use the top menu to enter the words that must appear in the title (Words in title), or you can use the name of the publication (Publication name), between quotation marks if it is a compound name. The latter option is obviously useless if you launch your search only on the Web by activating the World Wide Web button.

Northern Light			
	Search for		Search Tips
	Words in title		
	Publication name		See our list of publications.
	Words in URL		
	SELECT ⊙ All Sources ○ Special Collection ○ World Wide Web		

Home
Help Center
Accounts
About
Alerts
Portfolio

LIMIT SUBJECTS TO

☐ Arts   ☐ Gov't, Law & Politics   ☐ Social sciences
☐ Business & Investing   ☐ Health & Medicine   ☐ Sports & Recreation
☐ Computing & Internet   ☐ Humanities   ☐ Technology
☐ Contemporary life   ☐ Products & Services   ☐ Travel
☐ Education   ☐ Reference
☐ Entertainment   ☐ Science & Mathematics

LIMIT DOCUMENTS TO

☐ Commercial Web sites   ☐ Personal pages   ☐ Broadcast news transcripts
☐ Education Web sites   ☐ Learning materials   ☐ City & regional newspapers
☐ Government Web sites   ☐ Questions and answers   ☐ College newspapers
☐ Military Web sites   ☐ For sale   ☐ Newspapers, wires & transcripts
☐ Non-profit Web sites   ☐ Job listings   ☐ Press releases

The second part of the Power Search page enables you to specify the word or words that must appear in the address of the site (Words in URL).

LIMIT SUBJECTS TO enables you to restrict the scope of your search to one or more subjects. Just tick the subjects you want: **Arts, Business, Health & Medicine**, etc. Otherwise, the search will be carried out on all the subjects.

LIMIT DOCUMENTS TO enables you to refine your search even further by specifying the type of sites for the search: **Commercial Web sites, Education Web sites, Personal Pages**, etc. Otherwise, the search is carried out on all the sites.

The **Any language** drop-down menu enables you to define the languages of the sites you want. By default, the search is carried out on all the languages, but you can opt for English, French, German, Italian or Spanish.

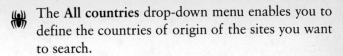 The **All countries** drop-down menu enables you to define the countries of origin of the sites you want to search.

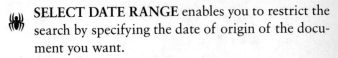 **SELECT DATE RANGE** enables you to restrict the search by specifying the date of origin of the document you want.

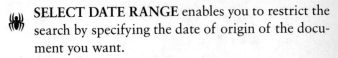 **SORT RESULTS BY** defines the order of presentation of the results. By default, they are presented according to their *relevance*. You can also activate the date criterion.

Remarks

On the left part of the results page, you will find the **Custom Search Folders** which group results according to subject, language, domain (commercial sites, personal pages, etc.) or content type (press agency dispatches, etc.). These folders are divided into subfolders, and if a site has many pages that correspond to your query, they too can be grouped in a folder.

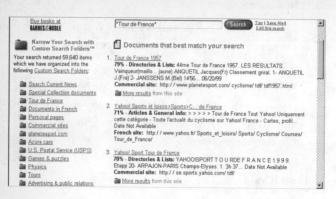

These folders enable you to pinpoint rapidly the results most likely to interest you, without having to go through all the pages that the search yielded.

 Under the address of a site, you will often see **More results from this site**. This link refers to you other pages at the same address.

On the home page, Northern Light features a search engine specific to the business world (**Business Search**), the stock market (**Investext Search**) and the news of the day or of the last two weeks (**News Search**). All three also contain highly sophisticated features.

 On the same home page, **Special Editions** enables you to conduct an advanced search on selected topics (European Economic Union, Linux, etc.) thanks to a choice of Web sites, articles or publications.

 Northern Light recognises the following field limiters: *title*, *text*, *url*.

Yahoo!

http://uk.yahoo.com

Yahoo is not a search engine proper, but a directory. The sites are indexed, described and classified by a team of IT experts, and are thus based on 'human' choices.

Developed in 1994 at Stanford University, Yahoo rapidly emerged as the directory of Web sites par excellence. Rare indeed are those surfers who have not included it in their toolbox.

The Yahoo database is not comparable with that of 'large' search engines, but it is of invaluable help when it comes to exploring a given subject.

Moreover, Yahoo offers a wide range of services and resources, including customisation of the home page, e-mail, news, selection of sites for children, auctions and classifieds.

Simple search

Two search methods are available. You can search either by entering keywords in the search form, or by proceeding through the categories and subcategories until you find what you want. If you want to find a specific item of information, use keywords, but if you want to explore a topic in a wider sense, you should proceed through the categories.

For example, if you are looking for information on an author such as Pinter, enter his name. If, on the other hand, you want to explore English literature on the Web, your search will be more complete if you proceed through *Art & Humanities* and *Literature*.

In both cases, Yahoo searches its database and yields results grouped into three fields: categories, sites and news dispatches. You will then find the relevant *Web pages* which are indexed by the Inktomi search engine.

If Yahoo finds nothing that corresponds to your query in its directory, it passes your search directly on to the Inktomi search engine, which explores the Web in full text, without going through the Yahoo directory.

By keywords

Enter the expression or keywords in the text field, and click **Search**.

By default, Yahoo searches for all the terms of the query, as if they were linked by AND. However, if a term must be contained in the results, put the + sign before it.

** assassination+Kennedy**

will yield no page which does not contain the term Kennedy and assassination.

 To restrict the search, enter a term with the minus sign (–) right before it.

** +Kennedy+assassination−Bobby**

will search for pages dealing with the assassination of John Kennedy, but not with that of his brother Bobby.

 To search for an exact phrase or expression, put it between quotation marks.

** 'New York Times'**

conducts a search on the title of the New York daily newspaper, not on the three terms separately.

🕷 To limit the scope of the search to the title or the URL, use the operators **t:** or **u:**

t:Kennedy

restricts the search to pages whose title contains Kennedy

u:Kennedy

restricts the search to pages whose address contains Kennedy

🕷 An asterisk (*) placed after a character string replaces between zero and several characters.

garden*

searches for garden, gardens, gardening, etc.

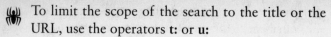

Do not enter keywords here. Instead, click on one of 14 categories and proceed by clicking subcategories.

For example, if you want information on the saxophone, you must proceed as follows: **Entertainment, Music, Instruments, Wind Instruments, Saxophone (3)**. The figure between parentheses indicates the number of subcategories that contain information on your subject. One of these may be followed by the @ sign, indicating that this category is also contained in another hierarchy. In our example, *Instrumentalists@* is also found in another category which contains violinists, accordionists, etc. as well.

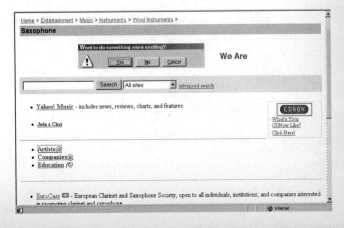

The two search methods yield results that will enable you to explore the pages or categories that contain them. Under these results, you will find the Web page links which refer you to the results collected by the Inktomi search engine.

Advanced Search

To access the **Search Options**, click on **Advanced search** in the home page.

The default search is carried out on **Yahoo**. Radio buttons under the entry window can be used to switch the search to the **Usenet**. This search is actually carried out by Deja News, the specialised newsgroups search engine.

```
Select a search method
```

The search method is not defined by default. In this case, you can apply the same method as when conducting a simple search, using quotation marks, +, –, etc.

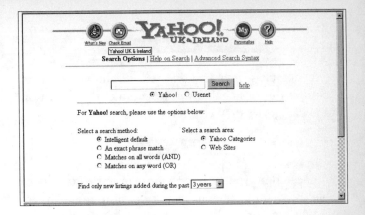

To search for a phrase or expression as if it were placed between quotation marks, select the option **An exact phrase match**.

To include *all* the keywords in the search, activate **Matches on all words** (AND).

To search for at least one of the words, click **Matches on any word** (OR).

Select a search area

The default search area selected is **Yahoo categories**. The other options enable you to conduct the search on **Yahoo categories** or **Web sites**.

New listings

You can limit your search to more or less recent documents. By default, they must not be more than 3 years old. You can limit the date to a day (for news, for example), 3 days, one month, etc.

Results display

The default display is set at 20 results per page. You can set it to 10 or 50 per page.

Remarks

Yahoo is not case sensitive.

A site with a logo representing dark glasses is considered a must in its category.

Under **Yahooligans!**, on the home page, you will find a large selection of sites for children, grouped by categories (Around the World, School Bell, Science & Nature, Sports & Recreation, etc.). The **Parents' Guide** includes Safety sites, Browsers for Kids, etc.

My Yahoo! enables you to customise your home page according to your areas of interest and thus obtain a Yahoo to suit your individual needs.

Below the results you will find links to other search engines. Click on one of them and your search will automatically be submitted to it. Unfortunately, the search options you have selected will not be recognised, however.

Specific UK search engines

http://www.searchuk.com

Designed in 1996, searchUK has emerged as one of the most important search engines for UK sites. Unlike many of the others, its home page is very succinct and goes directly to the point. The search is conducted by keywords or through any of the 21 categories.

It also features address or business search modules (**Find a business**).

Simple search

By category

Click the category or folder corresponding to your search. This search will present the list of subcategories. Each of these is followed by two figures. The first specifies the number of subcategories accessible and the second the number of sites contained. Continue clicking until you reach the subject you want, which will present a series of relevant addresses.

By keywords

🕷 Enter the keyword(s) in the search form and click **searchUK**.

🕷 To find documents that must contain one of the terms of your query, put the plus sign (+) without a space, in front of them.

+telecommunications Africa

will search for documents containing telecommunications and, by preference, also Africa.

🕷 To find documents containing all the terms of your query, link them with AND (with spaces).

telecommunications AND Africa

will search for documents containing the two words of the query.

To find documents containing at least one of the terms of your query, link them with OR (with spaces).

Asia OR Africa

will search for documents containing one of the terms of the query or both. The latter are placed at the top of the results.

 To find documents that do not contain one of the terms of your query, put NOT (with spaces) or use the minus sign (–) without a space in front of the term in question.

Telecommunications NOT Africa

or telecommunications –Africa

will search for documents containing telecommunications but not Africa.

 To find documents containing an exact phrase or expression, put it in quotation marks.

'mad cow disease'

will search documents containing the three words side by side but not separately from each other.

To find documents containing two terms near each other, link them with NEAR/*x*, where *x* specifies the maximum number of words between them.

'mad cow disease' NEAR/5 France

will search for documents where these two terms are not more than 5 words away from each other.

For more complex searches, use parentheses.

telecommunications AND (Asia OR Africa)

will search for documents containing *telecommunications* and at least one of the two other words.

Advanced search

To access the advanced search, click **Advanced Options**.

Display results enables you to specify the number of results to display per page as well as how detailed you want them to be presented. If you opt for **Detailed**, bear in mind that it will slow down the loading of the page.

Limit search to enables you to limit the search field. The default search is carried out on **All classes**, but other options are available: **Commercial sites** (.co, .ltd, .plc, .com), **Academic** (.ac, .sch, .edu), **Government** (.gov, .mil, .nhs) or **Non-profit** (.org).

Domain clustering enables you to change the number of consecutive results per domain (unlimited, or 1 to 5).

Grouping enables you to specify whether the results should be classified by order of relevance. The default option is **No grouping**. If you choose **By**

domain, the different pages of the same site will be grouped. **By Class** will group the pages by their class (.co, .com, .edu, etc.).

 Related words enables you to conduct your search using keywords related to your query which appear in the results page. By default, simply tick the word(s) you want to add to your query and click **Search**. The other option, **Show related words** launches a new search on the single ticked word, without including the words in your query. If you do not want searchUK to yield keywords, activate **Don't Show**.

 If you want to keep the selected options for a subsequent search, click on **use these settings next time**. This could save you time.

UK PLUS

http://www.ukplus.com

Launched by the Daily Mail & General Trust, this directory lists UK web sites in particular, but also sites from elsewhere if the UK Plus team considers them likely to interest British surfers.

The sites are grouped in categories or channels, themselves divided into subcategories. The home page features 20 main categories which include Arts/Humanities, Business, Computing and Education. These categories are subdivided into 2,200 subcategories.

Each site is visited by a specialised journalist who draws up a brief description of it.

For an extensive search on the Web, UK Plus is obviously not the ideal tool. Conversely, the quality of the selection and descriptions of the sites make it an interesting resource for exploring the UK Web.

Search

By categories

 Click on the category corresponding to your search. This link presents a list of subcategories representing the second level of the search structure. Continue clicking to limit the search field further until you reach the results page you want. If the description of a site corresponds to your search, click on this link to obtain the desired page.

> For example, if you are searching for information in the music field on stringed instruments, you will proceed as follows: Entertainment: Music: Instruments: Strings. This page then yields sites on the piano, the guitar, the cello, etc. Click on the title of one of them to access the home page of the site in question.

 At the bottom of each page, you will also find a form with which to launch a keyword search, so you don't have to go back to the UK Plus home page.

By keyword

(🕷) Enter the keyword(s) in the search form and click **Search**. The default search is carried out on the UK Plus database. If you want to carry out a search on all the Web, click on **All the web**.

(🕷) If you want the documents found to contain all the terms of your query, enter the plus sign (+) between them, without a space.

Turner+Whistler

will yield pages containing the names of the two painters.

(🕷) If you want the documents found to contain at least one of the terms of your query, enter OR between them, in uppercase, with spaces.

Turner OR Whistler

will yield pages containing one or the other name, or both.

To search for an exact phrase or expression, put it between quotation marks.

'National Gallery'

will search for pages containing the two words side by side, not distant from one another.

 For more complex searches, you can use parentheses.

(Turner OR Whistler)+'National Gallery'

will yield documents containing National Gallery and perhaps also Turner or Whistler, or both.

Remarks

 UK Plus is not case sensitive.

 If you click **All the web**, the search will be carried out by Infoseek UK.

 To be kept up to date on new developments, UK Plus invites you to subscribe to its Newsletter that will be sent to you by e-mail.

META SEARCH ENGINES

Meta search engines, or metasearchers, search more than one search engine at a time. They do not search on the Web themselves and do not have their own database. They are pieces of intermediary software that transmit your query to other search tools, engines or directories. Some 'translate' your query to bring it in line with the inherent features of each search engine.

They then yield the results gathered by the tools that have been contacted. The presentation of these results varies from one meta search engine to another. Some group them by search engine, others by relevance, eliminating duplicates.

Unity is strength. In querying several tools simultaneously you are obviously bound to benefit from the cumulative force of these search engines. Another advantage is that you save considerable time, carrying out a single search (albeit slower) rather than a successive one on these different engines. Furthermore, you can get a quick idea of their respective relevance for your query.

In addition, you must take account of the fact that the way in which you formed your query may not be recognised by one of these tools, each of which has its own search syntax. You cannot enter the advanced options of some search engines which enable you, for example, to restrict the search to a field, a date or a domain. It is also worth nothing that a meta search engine cannot physically yield all the results of each search engine that has been queried. You will find only the 10 or 20 first matches which, in theory, contain the most relevant results.

That said, for relatively simple searches, the meta search engines may prove of great help, and perhaps also lead you to discover efficient search engines you may never have used otherwise.

As the search features are reduced, it is all the more vital to choose the keywords of your search judiciously. A simple search with precise keywords will in any event yield better results than a sophisticated search with a vague query.

SavySearch

http://www.savysearch.com

Developed in 1995 by the University of Colorado, SavySearch was acquired by CNet Inc. in October 1998. It features an entry interface in 21 languages.

It can consult an impressive number of search engines and directories as well as specialised theme search engines. You can also gear your query to newsgroups, shareware, e-mail addresses, encyclopaedias, MP3, the children's Web, etc. The search itself is extremely fast.

Available tools

Search engines

AltaVista, DirectHit, Excite, Galaxy, Fast, Google, HotBot, Infoseek, Lycos, Thunderstone, WebCrawler.

Directories

eBlast, Clearinghouse, GoTo, LookSmart, Lycos Top, Magellan, Mining Co., Open Directory, PlanetSearch, Realnames, Snap, SurfPoint, Yahoo.

News

Infoseek News, Newsbot, News.com, NewsTracker News, Yahoo News.

Search

 Two buttons under the entry form enable you to specify your search method:

And launches the search on all the words of the query.

Phrase launches the search on the exact phrase or expression.

Search
Submit
Snoop
Customize
Savvynews
Tell a friend!

Welcome to SavvySearch!
» Enter your query in the form above to metasearch the major search engines and guides, or select one of the specialized metasearch or metashop categories below.

MSIE users:
Make Savvy your
default search!

Search	Specialty		Shop
Guides	Australia	Jobs	Auctions
News	Colleges	Kids	Baby & Child
Search Engines	Dansk	MP3	Books
Shareware	Deutsch	Magazine Articles	Electronics
Usenet	Domain Names	Movies	Flowers
	E-mail Addresses	Newspapers	Fragrances
	Education	Recipes	Hardware
	Encyclopedias	Sports	Magazines
	Español	Stock Discussions	Music
	Français	Television	Software
	Health	Travel	Spirits
	Horoscopes	Web Development	Toys
	Images		Video Games
	Investing		Videos
	Italiano		Vitamins

Translations: Français Deutsch Italiano Português Español Nederlands Norsk Hangul Russian Suomi Esperanto Svenska Nihongo Dansk Greek Slovensky Româna Slovenko Polski Cesky Hebrew Hrvatski Magyar

http://www.savvysearch.com/search   Internet

 Under **Search**, SavvySearch asks you to choose the type of search: **Guides**, **News**, **Search Engines**, **Shareware** or **Usenet**. The default search is conducted with search engines, as indicated above the entry

window, after *metasearch*. You can also browse through the categories under *Specialty*.

 To search for a phrase or body of text, put it between quotation marks. SavySearch authorises a Boolean search as well, with the operators AND, OR, NOT or the plus (+) or minus (–) signs, and will in theory adapt your syntax to that of each search engine. Parentheses are also accepted for more complex searches. However, the more complex your query, the less likely it is to be recognised by all the search engines.

Thus the query

+star +evolution –wars

will be recognised by more search engines than **star AND evolution NOT ('star wars' OR 'star system')** because not all search engines recognise parentheses.

🕷 SavySearch is not case sensitive.

🕷 SavySearch integrates all the results (classified by order of relevance) of the different search engines by indicating their origin. You can either go to the indicated page or continue the search on the indicated search engine.

🕷 In SavySearch you can also restart the search to query other search engines.

Remarks

The default search is carried out on a selection of tools 'adapted' to most queries, but SavySearch also features a very interesting customisation function that enables you to select the desired search tools. To access this function, click **Customize** on the home page. You can choose among some 100 tools grouped by categories (Search Engines, Guides, Usenet, Sharewares, Encyclopaedias, etc.). You can activate the ones that seem most appropriate and give them a higher or lower value. Then, simply enter a name that will enable SavySearch to conduct a search customised to your profile.

MetaCrawler

http://www.metacrawler.com

Designed in 1995 at Washington University, MetaCrawler is today part of the Go2Net. It can carry out a simple and an advanced search and with the latter you can specify the search engines.

The *channels* offer numerous resources on the selected subject and enable you to conduct targeted searches with specialised search engines.

General tools available

AltaVista, Infoseek, Excite, Lycos, WebCrawler, Thunderstone, About, LookSmart, GoTo, DirectHit.

Simple search

🕷 Three buttons under the entry window can be used to define the search method:

any will search for documents containing at least one of the terms of the query (equivalent to OR).

all (default) will search for documents containing all the terms of the query (equivalent to AND).

phrase will search an exact phrase or expression as if it were put between quotation marks.

🕷 Tabs can be used to specify whether the search will be carried out on **The Web** (by default), on the **Newsgroups** or on **Audio/MP3**.

🕷 Furthermore, you can use the plus (+) and minus (−) signs to include or exclude a term from the search, and you can put a phrase or expression between quotation marks.

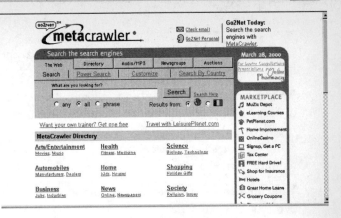

 Directory and Channels groups 20 categories (*Arts/Entertainment*, *Automobiles*, *Business*, *Computers*, etc.). You can either browse in the Open Directory, or click on one of the 10 *channels* which offer numerous resources on the selected subject, as well as specific search engines.

Advanced search

Click **Power Search** under the entry window in the home page.

Results from lets you specify the geographic field of the search. The default search is carried out on all the Web or all the newsgroups (**everywhere**). But you can also restrict it to a continent or a US domain (commercial, educational or governmental).

You can also specify the desired number of **Results per page**, **Results per source** or the search time (**Timeout**), which may vary from the **fastest** (default) to 5 minutes. If you define a fast value, the results of some search engines may not be included.

View results lets you specify whether the results are to be classified by **relevance** (the default value), by site or by **source** (search engine).

> Each result will be accompanied by a relevance rate, with 1000 being the optimal score.

The final option enables you to select the search engines that will carry out the search (AltaVista, Excite, and so on).

Remarks

Customize lets you customize the search grid according to the selected settings. You can thus carry out searches always with the same search engines, rather than letting MetaCrawler decide.

MetaCrawler does not wait for the results of all the search engines that have been queried. It suggests, after an initial search, to **Try again with longer timeouts**, so as to get lagging results.

For a lighter interface adapted to Lynx and to older browsers, click on **Low Bandwidth**.

The **MiniCrawler** function enables you to keep a mini-window on your desktop so as to start a search with MetaCrawler at any time.

ProFusion

http://www.profusion.com

The result of a research project conducted at the University of Kansas, ProFusion was launched in September 1998. Its extremely clear home page features an astounding number of search options that make ProFusion a very sophisticated tool. There is no 'advanced' search, but the features of the 'simple' search are more than sufficient to outperform other meta search engines.

It also has a useful feature that allows you to check deadlines.

Tools available

AltaVista, Excite, GoTo, Infoseek, Magellan, All the Web (Fast), LookSmart, WebCrawler, Yahoo.

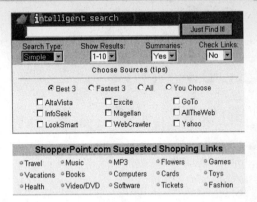

Search

Search Type lets you define the search method:

Simple (default) carries out an unspecified search.

All (AND) will search for documents containing all the terms of the query.

Any (OR) will search for documents containing at least one of the terms of the query.

(📑) **Boolean** lets you draw up a query with the Boolean operators AND or &, OR or |, NOT or !, NEAR or ~, and to combine them with parentheses:

> **(cat AND dog) NOT food**
>
> is equivalent to
>
> **(cat & dog) ! food**

(📑) **Results** specifies the number of results. The default value is 10.

(📑) **Summaries** gives you the option of a brief description of the sites (default) or not.

(📑) **Check Links** features a very rare function, i.e. it checks whether the pages are still active. There is no check by default, but you can activate this option and stipulate the number of links to check.

(📑) **Choose sources** is another interesting option based on artificial intelligence searches. By default, ProFusion chooses the three search engines that seem most suited to your search (**Best 3**).

If you are in a hurry, select **Fastest 3**.

All carries out the search on all the search engines. The search time will therefore be slower.

 You choose lets you decide which search engines to use by ticking the appropriate checkboxes.

Remarks

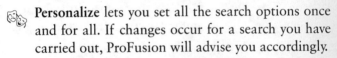

Personalize lets you set all the search options once and for all. If changes occur for a search you have carried out, ProFusion will advise you accordingly.

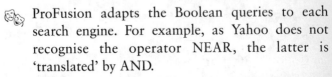

ProFusion adapts the Boolean queries to each search engine. For example, as Yahoo does not recognise the operator NEAR, the latter is 'translated' by AND.

Duplicates are eliminated from the results.

The results are classified by order of relevance, the top value being 1.0. The first page in the list may be rated as 0.987, for instance.

Copernic 2000

http://www.copernic.com

Developed by Agents Technologies, a company in Quebec, this meta search software belongs to the family of what are known as 'intelligent agents'. Unlike other meta search engines, Copernic 2000 is not consulted from a Web address but directly from your computer. You must in fact download it first from the address indicated above.

Three versions of the software are available, including one for free, which is the one we will consider here.

Copernic 2000 prides itself on being able to search more than 55 search engines grouped in six different domains. These search tools include the major general search engines and directories such as AltaVista, Euroseek, Excite, Fast, Hotbot, Lycos, Magellan and Netscape Netcenter.

In addition, Copernic automatically updates the search engines and software concerned.

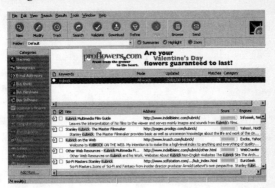

Search

First of all you select a domain (World Wide Web, newsgroups, e-mail, shopping for books, software or computer equipment) and then enter your query to conduct a simple search. Depending on the query, Copernic connects to the most relevant engines to conduct the search.

For a more complex search, another form features the options **All the words** (AND), **One word** (OR) or **Exact phrase**. Finally, an 'advanced' search lets you enter Boolean operators.

There is also a wizard to help you create searches.

Results

Duplicates are eliminated automatically.

The results are classified by order of relevance and the score of each is indicated in numeric or graphic mode.

Keywords are underlined in the titles and summaries, as well as in the downloaded documents.

Inaccessible or outdated documents may be deleted.

You can download several documents simultaneously to consult them offline.

The history of your searches is kept on your hard disk so that you can have them updated at all times.

 There are options for customizing the type of search (fast, normal, detailed, customized) and for presenting the results.

5

Specific searches

Arts

World Wide Arts Resources

http://wwar.com

This search engine claims to be the 'definitive inter-active' gateway to the world of the arts on the Internet. It enables you to consult a database of several hundreds of thousands of visited and selected sites. A brief description accompanies the sites, which are grouped into main sections: architecture, artists, galleries, academies, agencies/organisations, antiques, opera, dance, theatre, art history, etc. You can either browse through these sections or search by keyword.

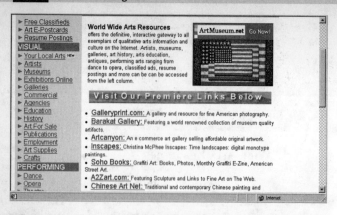

Cinema

The Internet Movie Database

http://www.imdb.com

This gigantic database on movies has become a film reference not to be ignored, with more than 200,000 films, 400,000 actors and actresses, 40,000 filmmakers and scores of technicians, scriptwriters and other related personnel listed. Searches by keyword are carried out by film title, actor, producer or character in a film. Biographies, filmographies, detailed credits, dialogues, criticism – it is all there! There are also listings on new films out, videos and a cinema glossary.

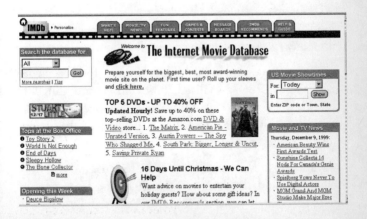

Dictionaries

On-line Dictionaries

http://www.facstaff.bucknell.edu/rbeard/diction.html

This is an extremely useful directory of dictionaries and thesauruses online. Most can be consulted free of charge, with a few exceptions, indexed here for their quality.

There are more than 800 dictionaries in 160 languages listed. General or specialised, bilingual or multilingual, glossaries, grammar summaries, crossword puzzle dictionaries, books of quotations – the choice is truly vast and constitutes a particularly appreciable tool.

Numerous dictionaries are devoted to information technology and the Internet, which is good for people particularly interested in IT and the Web itself. Others will appreciate the French – English – French Gastronomy Dictionary.

References are classified by language and divided into General Dictionaries and Specialized Dictionaries.

Afrikaans	Aklanon	Alabama	Albanian	Algerian	Amharic	Arabic	Arawakan
*Armenian	ASL	Avestan	Ayapathu	Aymara	Bantu	Basa	Basque
Belarusan	Bengali	Berber	Bobangi	Brahui	Breton	*Butuanon	Bukusu
Bulgarian	Burmese	Cantonese	Catalan	*Cayuga	Cebuano	Chamorro	Chechen
Cherokee	Chewa	Cheyenne	Chinese	*Ch'ol	Cispa	*Coptic	Creole
Croatian	Czech	Danish	Demonh'ka	Dutch	Eggon	Egyptian	Emakua
English	Eskimo	Esperanto	Estonian	*Etruscan	Fang	*Faroese	Farsi
Finnish	Frankish	French	Gaelic	Galician	Gaulish	Gamilaraay	Ganda
Gbari	German	Gevove	Gilbertese	Gothic	Greek	Guarani	Hakka
Halaka	Hawaiian	Hebrew	*Hiligaynon	Hmong	Hindi	Hungarian	Icelandic
Igbo	Indonesian	Ingush	Interlingua	Irish	Italian	Japanese	Jita
Kapampangan	Karelian	Katcha	Kerewe	Khmer	Kiga	Khowar	Klallam
Klingon	Kongo	Korean	Koyo	Kurdish	Lakhota	Latin	Latvian
Lenape	Lingala	Lithuanian	Lojban	Lozi	Luwian	Luganda	Lycian

Encyclopaedia

Britannica.com

http://www.britannica.com

Since the end of 1999, the Encyclopaedia Britannica has made its precious resources available to all surfers free of charge.

This work of reference par excellence is thus now literally at your finger tips. Enjoy it! It features a selection of 125,000 quality sites with commentary by experts, as well as a selection of articles from prestigious reviews. It is a site that in and by itself justifies the existence of the Web!

A query by keywords (with search options) yields the corresponding article in the encyclopaedia, related subjects and a selection of sites for a more in-depth search: an exemplary tool in every respect.

An excerpt from one of
the Encyclopaedia Britannica's Web pages.

Files

FILEZ

http://www.filez.com

FILEZ offers you a set of 75 million files to search and download. It rakes the Web daily and goes through more than 7000 FTP servers. You can browse in the four main categories (applications, games, desktop, MP3) with the Top 20 for each, or conduct a search using keywords by specifying the desired category (Windows, Macintosh, OS/2, Atari, MP3, Midi, graphics, etc.).

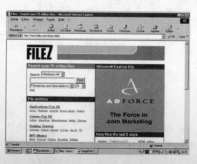

Theme Guides

WWW Virtual Library

http://vlib.org

This virtual library was launched by Tim Berners-Lee, the designer of HTML (hypertext language) and the Web itself. The principle is simple. Volunteers, most of whom stem from universities, undertake to create a directory of the best sites in their area of specialisation. In general, the sites selected are of very high quality and are accompanied by explanatory comments.

The search is carried out by keywords (with Boolean options), by categories or through an alphabetical index.

There are mirror sites in East Anglia (UK) and Geneva.

This is a reference for all those eagerly waiting for new in-depth information on a given discipline.

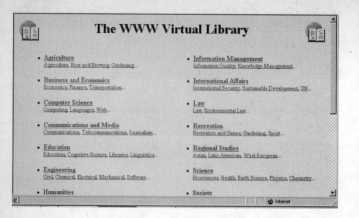

Argus Clearinghouse

http://www.clearinghouse.net

This is an access path to the best theme guides on the Web, classified by categories (Business & Economics, Communications, Computers, Humanities, etc.). You can conduct your search by keywords or by going through the theme chart. The only guides included are those that meet several criteria: description and evaluation of resources, presentation and organisation. A rating is attributed to each criterion and keywords give an indication of the contents of the guide.

This is another quality virtual library.

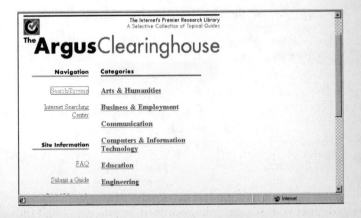

Images and video

Search engines such as AltaVista or Lycos (and to a lesser extent HotBot) also enable you to conduct this type of search. See the instructions for these search engines in chapter 4.

WebSEEK

http://www.disney.ctr.columbia.edu/WebSEEK

Designed in a Columbia University laboratory, this search engine tracks down images and videos on the Web. Two search options are available.

In the first, you enter a keyword that defines the object of your search. You can then launch a general search, or limit it to videos, colour photographs, black and white photographs or graphics.

The other option lets you proceed in one of the 16 categories and subcategories: animals (birds, dinosaurs, monkeys, etc.), architecture, art, astronomy, films, sports, etc.

The results are yielded in thumbnails with an indication of the size of the image. Click on the image to access the original page. With the Histogram command, you can even search for images in similar colours!

Search engines by country

International Directory of Search engines

http://www.searchenginecolossus.com

This directory gives you access to more than 1,027 search engines or directories by country. Directories produced by human search are in green, whereas search engines based on software robots are in white.

You can also find search engines grouped by theme (academic, business, Christian, hobby, music, sports, etc.).

Country Databases

http://www.internets.com/scountry.htm

A search by country features not only national search engines but also databases from the selected country. A drop-down menu also enables you to query search engines specialising in particular subjects. General databases on the countries of the world are also available.

Multimedia

Lycos RichMedia search

http://richmedia.lycos.com

Launched in November 1999 by Fast and Lycos, this new multimedia search engine can carry out simultaneous searches on images, videos and sound from a single query. A search on 'Star Trek' will yield, on the same results page, thumbnail images of videos to download and sound files in different formats. But you can also conduct your search on a particular medium.

Lycos features a catalogue of more than 17 million files. Other links let you conduct FTP or MP3 searches.

Music

MusicSearch

http://www. musicsearch. com

This search engine specialises in the music world on the Web and covers all types of music. More than 17,000 sites are listed with commentary. You can launch your search by entering one or more keywords or by using one of the categories (artists, musical event, file types, discussion groups, instruments, etc.). A more advanced search lets you specify the type of file (AU, MPEG, MIDI, WAV, POD, etc.) or the type of music (blues, hip hop, dance-techno, opera, funk, classical or religious music, etc.).

You can also launch a comparative search on CD prices.

Shareware

Shareware.com

http://shareware.com

Shareware are programs you can download directly from the Web. They are available in all fields (games, drivers, screen savers, utilities, etc.), and some outperform their commercial competitors.

This C/net search engine offers more than 250,000 shareware programs that you can locate and download by a simple or advanced search. You will have to specify your type of platform (Windows 95 or 98, Macintosh, Linux, OS/2, Unix, Amiga, etc.).

You will also find a list of most popular shareware, new developments or the editor's choices. Furthermore, you can subscribe to the newsletter to be kept up to date on this front.

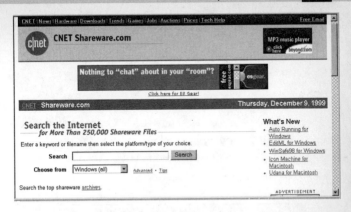

Radios

COMFM - Radio Guide

http://www.comfm.fr/radio/Live/indexa.html

Why not listen to the radio live on the Net, where you can log on to the entire world?

This directory offers you a choice of 2550 radios. You can search by country (USA, Canada, Lebanon, Moldova, China, etc.). There are some 57 radio stations for the UK alone (BBC radios 1 to 5, FM Gold, Galaxy, etc.).

Another option enables you to select radio stations via the type of music: alternative, background, dance-techno, hip hop, opera, jazz, classical, etc. You can also hear the latest news flashes from ABC, AP News or the BBC at all times.

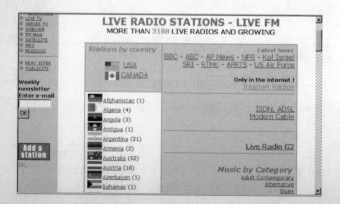

Business

Kompass

http://www. kompass. com

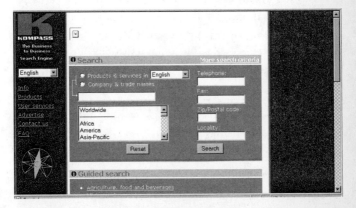

This is a search engine that enables you to find a company in an enormous database of more than 1.5 million businesses from the four corners of the world. The search is carried out either by company name, or by types of products and services (1700 in all). You can also specify the continent or select additional criteria.

The other option is to go through one of the 31 general categories (agriculture, food and beverages, mines and quarries, petroleum and gas, wood and furniture, textiles, telecommunication, transportation, health, etc.). This is a multilingual search engine for European companies only.

Europages, The European Business Directory

http://www.europages.com

This contains more than 500,000 European companies in 30 European countries. The search is conducted by product, service or by company name.

Europe

EuroSeek

http://www.euroseek.net

EuroSeek is a search engine for European sites. The home page features an interface in 40 languages. You have to specify whether the search is to be limited to a

given language or country, or to a particular field (companies, universities, organisations, governments, etc.). Various options are available for searching by keywords. The interface of each language offers links to local press organisations.

Other search engines for European sites:

Euroferret

> http://www. webtop. com

Yellowweb

> http://www. yweb. com

Information technology and the Internet

Webopedia

http://www.webopedia.com

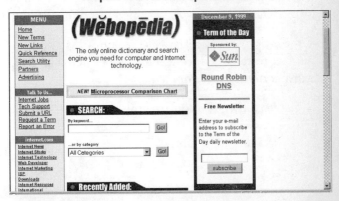

This is an online dictionary coupled with a search engine on the Web that include the terms, concepts and techniques of the information technology world. You enter the term you want in a given IT or Internet field, and Webopedia will give you the definition in hypertext, together with a series of pertinent links to deepen your knowledge. The definition of the term also provides a series of related terms to guide you to other definitions and sites. Web links are accompanied by comments and an evaluation.

Furthermore, Webopedia offers a newsletter to keep you posted on new developments.

A quality theoretical tool, that also provides practical information, Webopedia is an address you will wish to bookmark without a doubt.

NGOs, Sustainable Development, Human Rights

Oneworld.net

http://www.oneworld.org

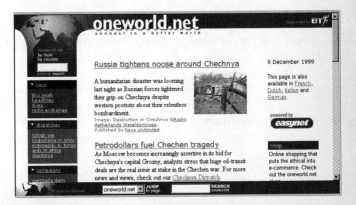

Oneworld is a network of several hundred non-governmental organisations (NGOs) involved in promoting sustainable development and human rights throughout the world. They include Oxfam, Save The Children, Action Aid and many lesser known organisations in the field.

In the search engine, you select the field of action (environment, human rights, news, etc.), the country (from Afghanistan to Zimbabwe) or the subject (agriculture, the arms trade, biodiversity, globalisation, conflicts, etc.).

It also features full references, analyses of ongoing conflicts, a photo gallery and a forum. In short, it is a very rich tool much appreciated by all those for whom government press releases do not provide enough information on the problems of the world today.

Webcams

EarthCam

http://www.earthcam.com

Webcams are small, digital cameras which, placed in Times Square or perhaps in front of your aquarium, broadcast images in real-time on the Web. They in effect turn us into global voyeurs. There are thousands all around the world.

In EarthCam, you can search by country, subject (animal, mountain, beach, etc.) or by category (beaches, bridges, towns, sports, adult, etc.). You can also consult a range of indexed categories (arts, space, sports, etc.).

Who knows, you might even find one staring at you in the workplace!

6

Index